TALKING ABOUT

Learning Difficulties

Sarah Levete

Franklin Watts
London • Sydney

© Aladdin Books Ltd 2006

Designed and produced by
Aladdin Books Ltd
2/3 Fitzroy Mews
London W1T 6DF

Printed in Malaysia

ISBN: 0-7496-6612-9

First published in 2006 by
Franklin Watts
338 Euston Road
London NW1 3BH

Franklin Watts Australia
Hachette Children's Books
Level 17/207 Kent Street
Sydney NSW 2000

A CIP record for this
book is available from
the British Library.

Design: Simon Morse;
Flick, Book Design and Graphics

Picture research:
Alexa Brown

Editor: Rebecca Pash

The consultant, Jill Davies, is
Research Programme Manager
at the Foundation for People
with Learning Disabilities. We
would like to thank Jill for
assisting with the learning
disabilities sections in this book.

Contents

"Why can it be difficult to learn?"

Some people find it easy to read or do sums while others may find it hard. Everyone struggles to learn some things, but there are often reasons why a person finds learning difficult. It may be to do with the way a person's brain makes sense of information. Or there may be problems at home or school that make it hard to learn.

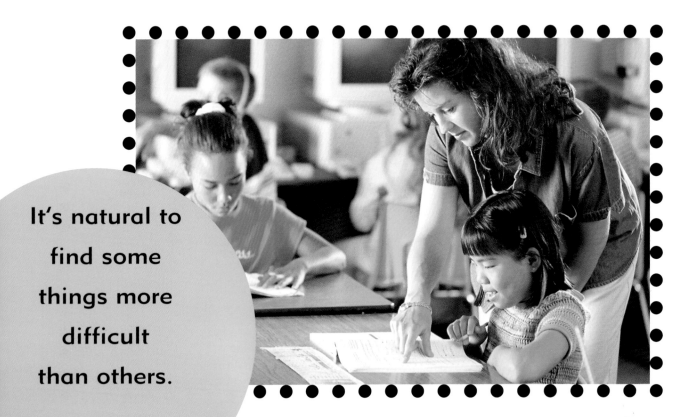

It's natural to find some things more difficult than others.

In this book, we talk about learning difficulties caused by the way the brain works and learning difficulties caused by problems at home or at school. We look at what it means to have a learning difficulty, how it feels and what can be done to make learning easier.

"What is a learning difficulty?"

A learning difficulty doesn't mean a person is not intelligent or able. It means that a person has particular difficulty learning and understanding some things.

For instance, a person with a learning difficulty may have trouble with reading and writing, but they may find it easy to learn other skills such as playing an instrument.

People with learning difficulties are often intelligent and gifted.

A learning difficulty is not an illness or a disease. There is no miracle cure but with extra support and different types of teaching, a person with a learning difficulty can learn fully.

Did you know…

A learning difficulty such as Attention Deficit Hyperactivity Disorder (ADHD for short) is caused by the way the brain works. It doesn't disappear, but there are things that can be done to make learning easier. Learning difficulties affect people in different ways, so teaching methods and support varies from person to person.

"Who has a learning difficulty?"

Look around. Any person you see could have a learning difficulty. You often can't tell just by looking at somebody. A learning difficulty can affect anyone, from any background or culture. It is often caused before a baby is born or while he or she is very young.

A learning difficulty doesn't stop a person from having a good job.

Many grown-ups have learning difficulties that they were born with. They are often able to manage their difficulty by focusing on their strengths and finding ways to overcome the things they find particularly difficult.

Did you know…

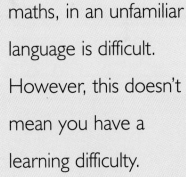

Many children speak English as a second language. They often speak another language at home. If your first language is not English, you may need extra help. Learning a new language and learning different subjects, such as maths, in an unfamiliar language is difficult. However, this doesn't mean you have a learning difficulty.

"What is dyslexia?"

You may have heard of the word "dyslexia". Many people have this learning difficulty. Dyslexia means "difficulty with words". A person with dyslexia may find it hard to see the words on a page clearly. Letters and words appear jumbled up. They may have difficulty with handwriting and always struggle to spell correctly.

Like other learning difficulties, dyslexia does not affect a person's intelligence. Dyslexia is caused by a difference in the part of the brain that deals with language.

Think about it

Look at these words. This is how the words may look to a person with dyslexia. It can be incredibly confusing!

incredibly confusing!
person with dyslexia. It can be
how the words may look to a
Look at these words. This is

Look at these words. This is
how the words may look to a
person with dyslexia. It can be
incredibly confusing!

"Is dyslexia just about words?"

Some people with dyslexia find it hard to understand numbers. It may also be hard to read and understand a map, to work out the direction of arrows, or to remember left and right. They may also find it hard to follow instructions.

Dyslexia can affect a person's ability to understand numbers, signs and instructions.

Signs of dyslexia can include:
• Seeing or saying words the wrong way round
• Difficulty tying shoelaces or doing up buttons
• Constant clumsiness
• Poor spelling
Remember, you may make spelling mistakes or struggle with buttons, but this doesn't always mean you are dyslexic.

Did you know…

Dyslexics are often very good at other things. From heads of major companies to poets and actors, many people are dyslexic. Tom Cruise and the famous chef, Jamie Oliver (right), are dyslexic. Even Einstein was dyslexic!

"What happens if you find learning difficult?"

If a parent or teacher thinks a child has a learning difficulty, a specially trained teacher asks the child to do some tests. The tests help decide if the child has a learning difficulty. It is important to find this out so that a child can receive extra help. There are often simple, practical things that can make learning easier, such as listening to tapes or being taught in small groups.

If you have a learning difficulty, you may receive extra help.

Children with special educational needs (SEN for short) have learning difficulties that make it particularly hard for them to learn. They often receive extra support or attend different lessons with special teachers. For some children, it may be better to attend a special school where more support is available.

My Story

"My brother Sam has ADHD (Attention Deficit Hyperactivity Disorder). This means he is always on the move, fidgeting and active. He can't sit still for long. Sam was always getting into trouble. But now they know what Sam has, he has extra help in the classroom and isn't always in trouble!"

Annie

"What kind of help is there for dyslexia?"

Dyslexia affects people in different ways. What might help one dyslexic may not help another. Placing coloured plastic over words can make them clearer. It may also help to listen to tapes, use flash cards or have information repeated several times. Being taught in a small group can help too.

There are many simple ways to make it easier for people with dyslexia to read.

At school, children are often given special lessons and extra time in exams. As dyslexics grow up, they usually find ways to deal with the things they find difficult. For example, they may use a computer spell-check when writing letters.

Think about it

In the past, children with dyslexia were thought to be "stupid" or lazy. No one knew they were dyslexic. These children had low opinions of themselves. Today, much more is known about dyslexia which means support and understanding are available when necessary.

"How does it feel to have a learning difficulty?"

Many people with learning difficulties are often very intelligent. This can lead to feelings of frustration as they are slowed down by problems in just one area.

It is important to remember that many people have learning difficulties and it is nothing to be ashamed of. It shouldn't make a person feel any less important or special.

A learning difficulty can make a person feel frustrated.

It can be especially hard if a learning difficulty is not identified. People may make ignorant and unkind remarks. At school, teachers may misunderstand a child and think he or she is rude or lazy.

Think about it

Imagine how it feels to be called clumsy or "stupid" when you are trying your best but need extra help. Imagine how it feels to struggle to see words clearly, or to be unable to concentrate for more than a minute.

"What about learning disabilities?"

Some children may have difficulties in all areas of learning. These children have "learning disabilities". They may need extra help with many things, such as eating and communicating.

Some children have a condition called autism which can affect behaviour and speech.

Autism can affect a child's ability to make friends and play with other children.

Someone with autism sees the world differently. This can make it difficult to communicate or understand other people's behaviour. The condition can get in the way with learning, but many people with autism lead independent and successful lives.

Did you know…

One of the most common learning disabilities is called Down's syndrome. Some babies are born with this condition. It affects their ability to learn but it does not affect their ability to play and laugh, just like any other child.

"Do physical disabilities make learning harder?"

A physical disability does not necessarily mean a person has a learning disability.

A person's physical ability is not related to his or her learning ability, but some conditions can affect how easy it is for a person to learn. For instance, cerebral palsy affects the way the body is able to move. A child with cerebral palsy will need a lot of extra help and may be unable to participate in some activities.

Cerebral palsy can affect parts of the brain involved in learning but many people with cerebral palsy do not have a learning difficulty – they may just need practical, physical help to sit up and join in lessons.

Did you know…

Being deaf or blind doesn't make a person less able to learn than anyone else. Practical support can make learning possible. Hearing equipment or books written in Braille (patterns of letters that you can feel) help a deaf or blind person overcome their physical disability.

"What other things can make learning hard?"

Many families are able to make sure that there is space and time to learn at home. But some children live in cramped, noisy conditions.

This can make it hard to do homework or to concentrate the next day. Many schools run special clubs where children can do homework.

It's not easy to learn when there is no space or time to concentrate.

If a pupil is always in trouble at school, he or she will find it difficult to learn. Disruptive behaviour may mean that a child is removed from lessons, or even expelled from school. Missing important lessons makes it difficult to catch up.

Think about it

If a parent or carer is very unwell, a child may need to care for them. This can also mean looking after younger brothers or sisters. Pressures such as these at home can make it hard to concentrate at school. If there are problems at home, talk to a teacher. He or she will understand and try to arrange some help for you and your family.

"Do learning difficulties disappear?"

A learning difficulty caused by the way the brain works, such as dyslexia, does not disappear. A learning disability such as Down's syndrome does not disappear. Difficulties caused by problems at home or school will disappear when the situation changes.

Learning disabilities do not disappear but they can be managed.

Learning difficulties caused by the way the brain works may not disappear but they can improve a lot with help. With support from family and school, most children with learning difficulties are able to manage their difficulty and become independent adults. A person with mild autism can probably do most things that other adults do. People with more severe learning disabilities may require support throughout life.

Think about it

Many grown-ups have difficulties with reading or writing. They may have missed out on schooling when younger or have had a learning difficulty that was never identified. These grown-ups often return to classes. This can help them find better jobs or help their own children with homework.

"What problems do people face?"

We all look different, behave differently, and learn differently. This is what makes life interesting. But some people are ignorant and unkind. They pick on people who have difficulties or who are different in some way. This is unfair and wrong.

It is never OK to pick on a person because he or she is in some way different.

It is important to think of and respect each person as an individual. For instance, think of someone's kindness, their lovely smile or how they are really good at doing jigsaws. A learning difficulty is only one part of a person's personality.

My Story

"I work in a bank and I have dyslexia. It was difficult at first. I felt like I worked slower than everyone else, yet worked twice as hard! Now, I've learnt how to do the job my way and I'm doing really well. My workmates were not very understanding until another workmate stood up for me. Now they accept me for who I am, a hard-working colleague!"
Sasha

"What can I do?"

If you think you might have a learning difficulty:

• Talk to parents and teachers.

• Don't hide away and hope no one will notice.

• Remind yourself of what you can do, not what you can't.

• Remember, everyone finds certain things difficult.

You can support people with learning difficulties by:

• Respecting a person for who they are.

• Understanding people have different ways of doing things.

• Making an effort to get to know someone who finds it hard to make friends.

A learning difficulty isn't something to be ashamed of.

Contact information

For further information on both learning difficulties and learning disabilities, try contacting these organisations:

The Foundation for People with Learning Disabilities
Sea Containers House, 20 Upper Ground, London SE1 9QB, UK
Tel : 020 7803 1100
www.learningdisabilities.org.uk

National Autistic Society
393 City Road, London EC1V 1NG, UK
Tel: 0845 070 4004 (10am-4pm weekdays)
info@nas.org.uk
www.autism.org.uk

The Bobath Centre for Children with Cerebral Palsy
Bradbury House, 250 East End Road
London N2 8AU, UK
Tel: 020 8444 3355
www.bobath.org.uk

Contact a Family
209-211 City Road, London EC1V 1JN, UK
Helpline 0808 808 3555
www.cafamily.org.uk

Down's Syndrome Association
153 Mitcham Road, London SW17 9PG
Tel: 0208 682 4522
www.downs-syndrome.org.uk

British Dyslexia Association
98 London Road, Reading
Berks RG1 5AU, UK
Tel: 0118 966 8271
www.bda-dyslexia.org.uk

MENCAP
123 Golden Lane,
London EC1Y 0RT
Tel: 0808 8081111
www.mencap.org.uk

Learning Difficulties Australia
PO Box 349, Carlton South, Victoria 3053
Tel: 03 8344 5361
www.ldaustralia.org.au

SPELD, Specific Learning Difficulties Federation of New Zealand
P.O.Box 25, Dargaville
Tel: 09-439-5955
www.speld.org.nz

There is lots of useful information about learning difficulties on the internet.

Index

Photocredits

The publishers would like to acknowledge that the photographs reproduced in this book have been posed by models or have been obtained from photographic agencies.
Abbreviations: l-left, r-right, b-bottom, t-top, c-centre, m-middle:
Front Cover, 6, 7br, 11, 17tl, 20, 23 – Photodisc. 1, 3tr, 10, 12 , 29tl– Corbis. 2, 3br, 7tl, 15 – PBD. 3mr, 9 – DAJ Digital Images. 4, 5, 14, 16, 25br, 30 – Brand X Pictures. 13tl, 17br, 19br, 22, 27 – istockphoto. 8, 29br – Imagesource. 13br – David Loftus. 18 – iconotec. 19tl – PBD. 21, 26 – Scovo. 24, 25tl – Digital Vision. 28 - Select Pictures.